CHAKRA & AURA CLEARING:

IMPROVE YOUR MENTAL AND PHYSICAL WELL BEING

MARION McGEOUGH

Published by Marion McGeough.

A CIP Catalogue record for this book is available from the British Library.

Formatting and cover design by ebook-designs.co.uk

CONTENTS

Chapter 1: A Quick Introduction	5
Chapter 2: What are the Chakras?	7
Chapter 3: The Root Chakra	13
Chapter 4: The Sacral Chakra	21
Chapter 5: The Solar Plexus Chakra	29
Chapter 6: The Heart Chakra	37
Chapter 7: The Throat Chakra	43
Chapter 8: The Brow Chakra	47
Chapter 9: The Crown Chakra	53
Chapter 10: Understanding the aura	57
Chapter 11: Chakra Clearing Meditations	65

CHAPTER 1: A QUICK INTRODUCTION

I decided to write only briefly here as I am sure that you will want to move forward and begin to understand more about the chakra system and how you can help clear and balance your chakras.

I have been interested in the chakra system for quite a while now. As a Reiki teacher I discovered that I could see other people's auras, especially after meditating. Curiosity led me to learn more about the chakra system. I really wanted to know the meaning of the colours that I saw, I was truly fascinated.

As you work through this book you will learn about each of the main chakras. Moving on, you will learn meditations that are powerful tools to help you balance and, if need be, unblock the chakra(s). Finally, you will learn about the aura: how to see the colours within it and how to unblock any negative energy that may reside within it.

As a result of all of your hard work you will feel better and more relaxed, centred and connected to others and the Universe. What better reward can there be?

Now, without any further hesitation, let us move forward together and learn about the chakra system.

Joy, love & light to you all

Marion

CHAPTER 2: WHAT ARE THE CHAKRAS?

The chakra system was developed in India over four thousand years ago and migrated to the West much later. As Yoga became popular many people, hungry for knowledge, became interested in studying Eastern ideas and concepts. It is now widely known and accepted that a chakra is a spinning disc or wheel which, for most people, spins in a clockwise direction. There are seven major chakras. These are found starting at the base of the spine and ending at the top of the skull. There are many minor ones which can be found in the feet, hands, finger tips and shoulders.

As a chakra spins it takes in energy from outside of the body. The energy is then assimilated within the body before being distributed around it. All living things are made up of light, energy and vibrations. Your chakra system is essential to maintaining your life force and vitality. The chakras spin at different rates with the lower chakras spinning slower than the upper ones. The lower chakras are concerned with day to day matters related to personal safety, security, having enough food and money for survival, pleasure and personal power. The upper chakras are concerned with matters of the mind such as thoughts and feelings, personal relationships, goals, hopes and aspirations as well as spiritual development.

A chakra will become blocked when the flow and distribution of energy is disrupted. This disruption can occur either quickly or slowly:

Quickly: If a person experiences a major life event, such as a bereavement or sudden shock. The chakra can become blocked as the person becomes withdrawn and tries to make sense of what has happened.

Slowly: Through childhood and adult experiences and observations which can lead to negative thoughts, and/or self-limiting beliefs, which occur over a period of time and have a compounding effect. As this effect is gradual the person themselves may not notice any changes; however, if the person was to meet someone that they do not see very often the change may be more apparent. A deep understanding of the human psyche and the ability to look within oneself are desirable skills to develop in order to address childhood events, experiences and traumas. At times, professional help is needed.

So, you now understand that a chakra can become blocked when there are, or have been, either changes in a person's external world, or changes in how a person perceives the world around them.

PRACTICAL EXERCISES

Below are 2 practical exercises to see how changes in your thoughts can affect how you feel:

Exercise 1
Find somewhere quiet where you will not be disturbed for a few minutes.

Before you begin please read the instructions below:

Think of the name of a film that had a sad or tragic ending that you remember quite well

Now think about that ending. It may help to close your eyes to help you focus. Set the scene in your mind as you think about who was there, what was said and what happened to make it such a sad ending

Open your eyes now

How do you feel?

If I could guess how you are feeling I would say that you are feeling a little down, perhaps even tired or irritable. You may also have begun to connect one negative thought with another. Perhaps you are already thinking of another film that had a very similar ending to the one you had just thought about.

Exercise 2
During this exercise I want you to think about something that made you laugh. This could be a funny film, a joke that someone told you or something funny that you did. Take your time really thinking about what you saw or what happened.

When you have finished ask yourself – how do you feel?

It is likely that you feel bright and uplifted and that you may even be thinking about other silly or funny events that have happened as your mind links one type of event with another.

These very simple exercises have shown that your thoughts affect your emotions. The way you think affects how you feel and this in turn affects the whole of the chakra system. If the energy or life force which is taken from the world into the chakra system becomes negative, this energy then begins to slow down the chakra and eventually block it. At the same time there is less energy, vitality and life force to distribute throughout the body.

Changes that occur within the physical body lead to a change in the person's emotional state. This change, in turn, affects how we think and how we interact with the external world. As the chakra becomes more and more blocked, changes occur within a person's behaviour and how they interact with the external world. Friends and family may challenge the person at times as their thoughts and actions become different to what others are used to. Physiological changes such as an altered breathing pattern, heart rate and metabolism may occur. If left unchecked the chakra may close down completely. If this happens the chakra above it will also become affected, eventually closing down as well and the whole process may continue throughout the whole of the major chakra system, resulting in illness/dis-ease.

I am sure we all know someone who we sense has shut down. Such a person is withdrawn, private – unwilling to discuss their personal thoughts and feelings and disconnected from the outside world. Such people are in a dark place. Life becomes hard, even when it may not be.

As you work through this book you will learn exercises that you can carry out to ensure that you maintain a good state of health and wellbeing and that you enjoy life and not just endure it. My wish, from my heart, is that you will become a being of light, energy and vitality.

CHAPTER 3: THE ROOT CHAKRA

The root chakra is found at the base of the spine. When looking at the order of the chakras, the root is considered to be the first chakra. Spinning at the slowest speed of all of the chakras, this one is a bright sparkling ruby red with shimmers of white light when perfectly balanced. If the chakra is blocked the appearance is somewhat different as the chakra then appears to be a muddy red.

The root chakra is concerned with our sense of security. When you think of the word root you may think of a tree of some sort, or perhaps a plant. When you think about a tree, allow your mind to wander to the roots of a tree. The roots are embedded deeply within the earth and are the basis for the solid foundations of the tree for the rest of its life. Damage to the roots will cause damage, or even death, to the tree itself.

In the same way that the roots of a tree can be damaged if not planted correctly, a baby can become psychologically harmed if the baby experiences a traumatic birth, or if the baby is rejected by the mother. When a baby is born its awareness is focused on its bodily functions and that of survival. A baby is only initially aware of its own need for nourishment and warmth and the baby cries in order to have its needs met. If the care given to the baby at this crucial time is not met then sadly the baby may die. Just as the young, immature roots of a tree may die if it does not receive water and adequate conditions to prosper.

Most babies fortunately do survive, as does the need for security that is deeply embedded in all of us. A sense of belonging and having a place in a loving family is essential to a person's health, no matter how old they are.

All the information we take in through our senses is stored deeply in our subconscious mind; the child, who as a baby failed to have its needs met will, over time, develop a deep need for security and not really know why. This need will begin to manifest itself when a person becomes an adult. As an adult, life can become complicated and so can our needs. Whilst we all have a basic requirement for food, shelter and clothing, having those needs met for some people is not enough. If a person has a deeply embedded sense of insecurity they may be driven to achieve more. Having more money, a bigger and better home and expensive clothing will do little to satisfy the deep need for security.

In many cases, having an abundance of money and material goods will heighten a person's sense of insecurity because they will become worried that someone will take it all away from them, or they will somehow lose everything. I have seen clients who outwardly appear to be successful and this success is achieved through hard work and commitment. However, in the initial stages of therapy the client will not be able to accept, or even recognise, that they are worthy and deserving of their success. A lack of security affects them on a deep psychological level. Often the person does not feel deserving of the success they have and may attribute it to good luck, someone's poor judgement, or they may feel very anxious and have a feeling that everything will tumble down around them because they will be "found out".

For some the opposite is true. If a person, who did not have their needs met as a baby, finds

gh life events and through
.ces to have those needs met in
, they may simply give up because
vince themselves that they are not
wo y and deserving of what life can give them. The result of this is a downward spiral.

Childhood, adolescent and adult experiences will impact on a person's sense of security as well. I have known clients who have had a happy and prosperous upbringing only to find that through life events such as a loss of a job, a bad investment, divorce or illness they have fallen on hard times.

Another way that our sense of security can become compromised is through learnt behaviour. If we are brought up in a family where the focus is on money, or a lack of it, then the child will internalise this behaviour and begin to focus its attention in the same way.

Too much energy in the root chakra will result in too much energy within the body. Such a person will find that even though they desire some life changes they are unable to commit to them, or begin to make those changes in the first place. The need for security can be so great that even the slightest change in routine can lead to emotional turmoil. A person with too much energy in the root chakra will be critical and judgemental of others; this criticism is a result of their own frustration and perceived inability to make plans and follow them through.

A lack of energy in the root chakra can often be seen in people who take little time over their appearance and tend to live in their heads. These people pay more attention to their spiritual needs. I am sure we all know someone like this: a person who is very quiet and who will do anything to deflect attention away from themselves on to something, or someone, else at any given opportunity. Individuals with a lack of energy in the root chakra think that they are insignificant to such an extent that even during therapy they sit curled up in a ball, often speaking in a quiet voice which is little more than a whisper, trying to use up as little space as possible by keeping their movements and responses to questions to a minimum.

An imbalance in the root chakra occurs as a result of fear. Whilst the emotion of fear is necessary to either stop us or motivate us to

an also lead us to our own
a prison of the mind, a prison of
which prevents us from seeing how
ally are.

Illnesses related to a root chakra imbalance

- Lower limb problems
- Sciatica
- Hypertension
- Immune system disorders
- Chronic fatigue
- Eating disorders
- Bowel disorders
- Paralysis of the body and mind – unable to move forward and make decisions

As the chakra becomes imbalanced due to too much or too little energy, the above mentioned conditions may become apparent. Immune system disorders, chronic fatigue and hypertension are as a result of the body being in a high state of alertness ready to deal with whatever problems arise.

As adults, if our needs are not met, we focus all our energy on the problem and run our minds over possible solutions time and time again. If we have financial problems we may look at ways to save money, earn more or cut down on what we already spend, even if it is very little. This constant focus on one aspect of a person's life leads to a depletion of energy and resources which often leads to a supressed immune system. Hypertension is due to the heightened state of alertness and the person's inability to cope.

Eating disorders are common with individuals with an imbalance of the root chakra. Feeling unworthy of food and being unable to meet their own needs, disconnected from the world and their roots a person may develop anorexia and or bulimia. Binge eating is a way of filling up the body to try and create a heaviness and connection to their roots.

Sciatica and lower limb problems are often present when there is an excess or deficiency of energy in the root chakra. Such conditions are often one of the first signs that there is an imbalance in this area.

Bowel problems occur as a mechanism of the subconscious need to hold on to waste as a personal possession. Constipation may occur when there is too much energy and diarrhoea when there is a deficiency of energy.

A person with a well balanced root chakra

- Can deal effectively with problems
- Focuses the majority of the time in the present
- Physically moves freely and easily (provided there are no other illnesses/diseases present to prevent this)
- Eats a balanced diet and maintains a healthy weight without self-imposed restrictions and feelings of guilt.
- Has regular, what is considered to be "normal" bowel movements most of the time.

CHAPTER 4: THE SACRAL CHAKRA

The Sacral chakra is the second major chakra. It is situated between the navel and the base of the spine and is concerned with our pleasure and sexuality. The colour of this chakra is bright orange and when functioning at its best the chakra appears to be bright orange with some streaks of white light shining through it.

The development of this chakra begins between the ages of 6 months and 2 years old. At this age a child begins to seek pleasure in a variety of ways. The young child likes to experience the pleasure of eating foods that they enjoy and these are often sweet tasting foods. At times the child will put things into its mouth, curious as to what the object will taste like. Often the child will quickly spit the object out as the resulting taste is less than desirable. A child will seek pleasure in many other ways; such as through play, watching television and exploring.

As we become older our opportunities to derive pleasure in life are reduced. We become busy with day to day living. Time is taken up with working, carrying out chores and sleeping. For many there is little pleasure in life other than the few hours that can be spared for watching the television. Most of us become wage slaves, committed to paying large mortgages and bills. For those that have been in a previous relationship that has produced children there may be child support to pay as well. What is ironic is that each of us, on a spiritual level, seeks freedom, but we are instead committed to many years of paying mortgages and bills as we seek to pay for our homes, our very own four walled prison, which we commit ourselves to as we become older and more frail, afraid or unable to venture far outside.

Is it any wonder then that, for many of us, the second chakra becomes compromised? As adults we need to experience pleasure just as much as a child does. Each of us needs to be touched in order to feel connected. This connection is necessary so that we can relate both to each other and with the world around us. If we are not touched we will shrivel up and die.

The sensation of touch is not necessarily of a sexual nature. We can hug our friends and family, experience a connection and feel much better for it. We can stroke an animal and feel much calmer and more relaxed. It is now widely believed that when elderly people spend some time petting animals the senior person's blood pressure is reduced and they experience a lovely sense of well-being. Sexual contact and sexual relationships are also necessary to enable a person to feel wanted and whole. Bonding and connection give each of us a place in society.

As adults we also seek pleasure in food. We eat things which are not necessarily good for us such as sweets, chocolate and cakes. Due to social pressures and expectations some of us develop eating disorders, or try to hide what we are eating. At times some people end up eating in secret. People do this because they feel guilty and guilt is the major emotion that affects the optimal functioning of the sacral chakra. Guilt can be an amazing driving force leading us to correct something we have done wrong, but it can also be used to drive us further forward on our path towards addiction, not only to food, but towards alcohol and/or other substances.

There are other ways in which we can become addicted. These ways may initially appear to be beneficial to us, but we need to take care because addiction may quickly follow. If we stop, or have to reduce what we are doing, the level of guilt can be overwhelming. Examples of such addictions include exercise and domestic chores. Whilst moderate amounts of exercise are good for us, if we have to miss a class, run or session and we worry about it to such an extent that we feel consumed with guilt, then this is an unhealthy habit. The same may be said for household chores. If we are unable to carry out the chores as planned we may feel that we do not have any control over our lives; we feel full of guilt about not carrying out the required task.

A person with a lack of energy in the sacral chakra will move in a rigid manner. This rigidity also affects the mind, as such a person fears change and disruption to routine. Having everything in its place and a place for everything would be an ideal motto for a person with a deficient sacral chakra.

Whilst it is preferable to be organised, clean and tidy, it is the way that a person reacts when things are not as expected that is important. A person with reduced energy in the sacral chakra will become overwhelmed and, in some cases, unable to function if things are not how they should be. In order to live life in this state of imbalance, those with a deficient sacral chakra will be socially inadequate and feel isolated due to this. A deep feeling of emptiness is often felt due to a lack of connection to others and the world around them.

Those who have too much energy in the sacral chakra, on the other hand, will feel a deep connection to other people and all that is around them. Whilst it is good to feel connected, those with too much energy in this area will discover that they are able to connect too deeply and will find that they feel others emotions too readily. At times even watching the news may bring such a person to tears as will watching an especially sad or happy movie. It is wonderful to have empathy for our fellow humans, as well as for animals and nature, however, it is when we feel too much that we need to take steps to balance our sacral chakra.

Illnesses associated with a sacral chakra imbalance

These can be classified into 3 major groups:

Addictions

- **Drugs/substances abuse**
- **Alcohol**
- **Food, either too much or too little**
- **Sex**

Mental Health problems

- **Depression**
- **Anxiety**
- **Anger issues**

A person with a lack of energy in the sacral chakra may find that they have low self-esteem. This reduced sense of self-worth leads to anger and depression in those individuals who secretly aspire to change their lives, but are unable to due to self-limiting behaviour. A person with a deficient sacral chakra will often withdraw from society. This behaviour will turn others away from them, reinforcing the belief that they are worthless. This type of behaviour can lead a person down the path of totally withdrawing from society.

A person with excess energy in the sacral chakra is also likely to develop problems. Those with an excess of energy in the sacral chakra can find that due to their trusting, giving nature, they are easily taken advantage of financially and/or emotionally. It would be really great if everyone had good intentions all of the time but, unfortunately, that is not the way that the world works and people do get taken advantage of.

Physical health problems

- Problems with circulation especially in the legs
- Kidney problems
- Urinary tract problems
- General aches and pains

ɲn with a well- balanced sacral chakra

, over indulge at times without ɪeeling guilty

- May like routine but can adapt to change easily
- Can communicate effectively
- Forms relationships easily
- Takes pleasure in nature
- Listens to other people and can be flexible in their opinion

CHAPTER 5: THE SOLAR PLEXUS CHAKRA

This chakra is situated just below the sternum. Appearing bright yellow in colour with white light shining through it this chakra, when well balanced, resembles the sun. When the chakra is imbalanced, the colour changes to that of a muddy yellow with patches of brown.

The solar plexus chakra is related to our sense of power. Our sense of self begins to develop between the ages of eighteen months and four years old; this is the age at which we begin to recognise that we are an individual, that we are separate from our mother/carers. At this age the child begins to recognise that it has free will and this is the age at which the child will start to test the parental boundaries by defying the parent's instructions in order to (subconsciously at times) establish the consequences of their actions.

This is why consistent and fair parenting is important. The child will become confused if on one occasion the parent says that the child can have some sweets from a shop on the way home from school and on another occasion the parent says that the child cannot have the sweets. The child is more likely to become angry if they are not told why they are unable to have something that they had a few days ago. For the child everything is the same so, when in the same situation, in the child's mind the parent should respond the same. From the parent's point of view they may feel that the child has had too many sweets, or the child has misbehaved and the treats are not to be forthcoming, or it may be that the parent is unable to afford the sweets.

Whilst there are a multitude of reasons why the child does not get what the child wants, in his/her mind there is anger due to the loss of power and control over what they want. This is how the brain works; if an adult or a child is not given an explanation they will use what information they have available and create one for themselves.

Children develop their sense of self-esteem, their sense of self-worth, from those around them. If the child is brought up in a loving and caring home it is likely that the child will develop into an adult who is well grounded and has a sense of who they are and what they would like to do with their lives. Many children are brought up in a family that fight a lot of the time. Some children are abused or neglected. Children who endure such experiences can find it much more difficult to establish their place in society.

As adults we find that many people may have power over our lives. The most obvious one is our employer. Other people who have power include family members, such as our partner, or even our parents. The use of the word 'power' should not exist in the latter forms of relationships. If you feel that your partner has power over you then you do not have an equal relationship. If your parents have power over you then this is a form of manipulation. In both of these relationships, if you do not do something that the person wants you to do, you end up feeling bad, guilty and worthless. Feeling this way does not lead to a good quality of life and a well-balanced solar plexus chakra.

A person with an excess of energy in the solar plexus region will find that they are constantly doing and achieving but do not feel satisfied.

Often these people will be in positions of power due to their wealth or power over others, as they are often business owners with employees. This excess of energy is achieved, in most cases, to make up for the loss of power in earlier childhood, but for others it is due to a major life event as an adult. Individuals with an excess of energy in the solar plexus chakra can become obsessed, not only with the power they themselves hold, but with other powerful people including world leaders and powerful states or countries. This sense of power is fuelled by a terrible fear – that of being controlled by other people. Some people in mundane jobs with an element of power thrive on using that small amount of power over others, but deep down they are deeply unhappy with their lot in life.

A lack of energy in the solar plexus region results in a quiet timid person who also looks to others for validation. Control of their life is given over to others as is their destiny.

Illnesses associated with the solar plexus chakra

- Chronic fatigue

- Depression
- Low self esteem
- A victim mentality
- Eating disorders
- Low blood sugar and diabetes
- Stomach problems such as bloating
- Digestive problems
- Liver problems

Often someone who has a sluggish solar plexus chakra will develop aches and pains to begin with as the body cries out for attention. Although medical attention is often sought there is found to be no underlying cause. This often manifests when the individual is tasked with something that they do not wish to do, or something that bothers them in some other way, such as going against their core values or something that puts a financial burden on them. This happens equally amongst the sexes.

An individual may feel exhausted working and caring for the family. Some have placed themselves under financial strain as there may not be enough money to go round. Along with the aches and pains which occur when a person says ‘yes’ when they really mean ‘no’ to something, the individual will begin to move at a sluggish and slow pace. As time moves forward, the movements become ever more painful and some people begin to resort to using wheelchairs, or not going out if they can help it. This social isolation can move a person that one step further into a cycle of depression. The lack of human contact and the pain, which is very real to the individual, has a draining and aging effect on them. Painkillers offer little relief.

Low self-esteem occurs with individuals who have been taught, or who have learnt due to how they have been treated by others, that they must always put others before themselves. Resentment can set in if a person does not have any, or has only a little, time for themselves as they are often caring for, or doing things for other people.

We all need some ‘me time’ when you do something for yourself that brings you joy. This is not being selfish as it is your fundamental right to invest in you. If this is a major issue for you then please be brave. You have already taken the first step by reading this book. Now go that little bit further by working on yourself to help balance the solar plexus chakra.

Physical problems occur when you internalise your emotions. Stomach problems and bloating are common symptoms of someone who has an imbalanced solar plexus chakra. As the individual keeps many of their emotions to themselves, this then has an impact on the body. One of the ways in which the body reacts is to try to push or to stuff emotions down – for some this is what they literally do. Overeating and other eating disorders are ways in which we deal with our feelings when we feel unable to express those feelings. For some, eating sweet foods is the only way they can find to "reward" themselves. This is, of course, not a reward as too much food which is rich in sugar and fat can cause a number of health problems.

A person with a well-balanced Solar Plexus Chakra

- Can say no without feeling guilty
- Takes time to enjoy life

- Has a well-balanced diet and does not feel guilty when, on the odd occasion they over indulge
- Has feelings of empathy at the appropriate time but does not get overly upset if not directly affected
- Is confident in verbally expressing their feelings
- Lives within their means financially
- Moves easily and feels comfortable within their body

CHAPTER 6: THE HEART CHAKRA

The heart chakra is found in the middle of the chest. This chakra represents the integration of body and mind. Spinning at a medium to fast pace, this chakra appears as a beautiful emerald green when it is balanced and a muddy green when not.

The heart chakra is concerned with our relationships with others and, most importantly, our feelings. How we feel about others and how we perceive they feel about us is of utmost importance. As children, the relationships that we create with our parents are the foundation upon which we base many of our other relationships. If we can feel the unconditional love from our parents and if we are treated with respect, whilst at the same time understanding that there are boundaries and rules to follow in life, then it is likely that we will be able to bond and form quality relationships with others.

If, however, we learn that in order to be worthy of love we must act in a certain way and achieve specific goals, then we learn that what we believe to be love has conditions attached and we become fearful and reject all forms of love.

Adults who suffered a family break up in childhood often have problems bonding with others. Difficulty bonding can also happen if one of the parents has died. The age that a child loses a loved one is important in helping to understand how the child will cope with the loss. Very young children may not understand what has happened, or even be aware that a parent has died. Older children and teenagers will understand what has happened but they may have difficulty working through the grief process. Professional advice should be sought in the majority of cases as other family members have their own grief to work through and do not have the professional skills necessary to help the child.

It is only in recent years that bereavement therapy has become available to children and, therefore, there are many adults who as children were simply left to work through the bereavement process alone. Many become stuck at a certain point, the heart chakra becomes blocked and this affects the individual in many ways. As adults, if we are unable to express our emotions fully the heart chakra will become blocked. Simple intuitive decisions from the heart are difficult and, at times, impossible due to the blockage.

Connecting with people in our daily lives, and understanding ourselves and others, are all emotions which come from the heart and these emotions lead to feelings, the feelings to actions. When the heart chakra is blocked, as with any of the other chakras we are unable to function as we should. We lose the ability to connect with others and the ability to relate to our own feelings. This is because we lose touch with our emotions. The loss or reduction of the ability to feel, empathise and forgive, as well as the ability to feel happiness and joy in our hearts, has a huge impact on how we live our lives and how we relate to others, as well as how others perceive and relate to us.

Illnesses associated with the heart chakra

- Low mood and depression

- Asthma and other respiratory diseases and disorders
- Heart disease
- Anxiety

As the heart chakra becomes blocked a person will often know that something is wrong but not know what the problem is. In order to begin to feel something individuals begin to take on bad habits, such as excessive eating or some may stop eating altogether, some may begin smoking. These are all habits some people adopt so that they simply feel something.

Anxiety, low mood and, in some cases, depression occur when the chakra is very imbalanced. Events of the past and worry about the future can result in mental health problems. Once the chakra is unblocked, and the individual begins to feel their true emotions, the need for the continuing bad habit is reduced and even eliminated in some cases.

A person with a well-balanced heart chakra

- Seeks quality, long term relationships
- Is confident in making decisions

- Sees personal satisfaction of primary importance
- Can express own emotions even at difficult times
- Has a balanced view on most things

CHAPTER 7: THE THROAT CHAKRA

Imagine a beautiful sunny day. The sky is a lovely shade of blue and everything seems just right with the world. A clear, balanced throat chakra is the same colour as that of a beautiful sky. The throat chakra is concerned with our ability to communicate and if we are prevented from doing this the chakra will become blocked.

In some cultures children are encouraged to express themselves and their opinions are allowed even at a very young age. Children in such cultures are often allowed to make their own choices related to what they wish to eat and what they wish to wear, often with some parental guidance. Being included in the decision making process and being allowed to choose gives a child some autonomy, the child feels important and part of the family. Other cultures believe that the child must be seen and not heard. The child is simply a child which needs to be directed. Children who find that they have had the ability to communicate restricted often develop difficulties with communication and this continues into adulthood if the issue is not addressed.

We all have to express ourselves and to make our needs known. Those of us that are unable to communicate verbally due to a disability will find some other ways to communicate. As adults, most of us are aware of what we say around specific people, such as the boss. Sometimes we feel as if we are bullied by an employer, or by a parent, or a partner at home. Being told to be quiet, being told that you are stupid or, when you do have the courage to speak up, being told that you don't know what you are talking about can have a deep psychological impact on a person. A person's self-esteem can be seriously affected. Such an individual may also feel withdrawn and may become depressed. Other emotions often surface such as anger and hate. These emotions can often build up through the months and sometimes the years and, as time passes by, the chakra becomes increasingly blocked.

I know a lady who had a very strict upbringing. Her father even chose the clothes she would wear to each and every occasion and this continued into her teenage years. As a result this lady now wears bright and flamboyant clothing. To someone who does not know this person she can appear to be a little crazy, wearing odd patterns and colours; however, I look beyond this as I know that this is really her way of saying "I am free at last – this is really me".

Sarah, another client, had problems speaking to other people. She was often told that she talked too much as a child and that what she said was just rubbish. As an adult she now chooses her words carefully and precisely, she does not engage in easy casual conversation and to many she may appear to be standoffish, but I know that she often feels afraid to speak in case she says something that is perceived to be "wrong". Whilst Sarah feels careful about what she says, there are other people who are totally the opposite and say anything and everything that comes into their minds. This occurs when there is an over stimulation of the throat chakra.

Common Illnesses associated with the throat chakra

- Thyroid disease

- Asthma
- A sore throat
- Anorexia
- A speech disorder
- Throat cancer
- Mouth ulcers

A person with a well- balanced throat chakra

- Has clear speech
- Talks at a moderate speed – speech is not rushed or too slow
- Enjoys public speaking
- Does not see the need to engage in gossip and is not malicious

CHAPTER 8: THE BROW CHAKRA

The brow chakra, or the Third Eye, refers to the area between the eyebrows. This chakra is indigo blue with some purple. This chakra develops throughout your life, as you are constantly learning and taking in information which is assimilated and understood. In adulthood a person may develop a midlife crisis if there is a big difference between what they believe to be true of the world and what has happened in their lives. If a person is not living the life that they thought that they would the Third Eye can become compromised. There are two aspects to the Brow Chakra. The first is your ability to look at yourself and your ability to assess your own actions in life so far and how those experiences will affect you in the future. How well do you know yourself? The second is related to your psychic ability. How willing are you to open yourself up to what is really there?

If you close your eyes now and concentrate on the area of the Third Eye you may feel a tingling or a buzzing sensation. Some people are able to see the shape of an eye, which may be open or half closed. If the eye is half closed it simply means that the individual's psychic and intuitive ability is reduced. As children many of us were told not to be silly, or our comments were ignored if we talked about intuition, insight and psychic abilities. People who believe in reincarnation suggest that those that have a half open Third Eye have consciously closed down half of the eye due to fear of being called witches and being persecuted.

The Third Eye is all seeing and all knowing. The Third Eye is able to record the events of your past and predict the future. As the Third Eye turns inwards this indicates that the answer to our questions lies within each of us. Our perceptions and belief system are held within. The way we appear to others is not always the way that we see ourselves.

If we spend most of our days engaged in work, chores and other activities, then we are spending most of our time doing things. This takes us away from who we are and what we really want in life. A person might feel that something is wrong, but not really know what the problem is. Feelings of isolation and of being disconnected can lead to a person questioning their purpose in life and, indeed, life in general.

I have done this myself and I have concluded that, in order to establish answers to such deep questions, a person has to spend time alone, looking deeply and uncritically within. This is not an easy task to accomplish and one must be patient and willing to learn who they really are. A person must take time to think about past life experiences and the way that those experiences have shaped who they are now.

Past thoughts and plans should also be considered. Whilst we all have past desires and ambitions from our youth, as adults we can look at these critically and decide those that were just childhood dreams and those that are possible and achievable with some planning, ambition and dedication. Many of us have wished to become a footballer or a supermodel but do not, and never will have, the skill or the looks to achieve that goal!

The Brow Chakra can become blocked and imbalanced as we become disconnected with who we are and what we want to do with our lives. There are times when we need to be realistic. If you enjoy painting, for example, but know that your work is not really good enough to make a living from, then it is no use leaving the day job to follow a career as an artist.

The Brow Chakra can become blocked when we are unable to move on from events in the past. The Third Eye has seen the past and this information is recorded in our memory, deep within our subconscious mind. What we have seen and done is never forgotten and this information subconsciously affects our decisions and behaviour and can prevent us from moving on with our lives.

Meditation and insight into our own behaviour will help to unblock the chakra. When the chakra is perfectly balanced an individual will be able to think more clearly, make well informed and organised decisions and have the ability to better understand their own actions and behaviours.

Illnesses associated with the Brow Chakra

- Tension headaches
- Visual problems
- Insomnia
- Sinus problems

Some mental health problems: anxiety and depression due to uncertainty and lack of clarity/direction

As the Third Eye becomes progressively imbalanced the illness becomes worse. Headaches will increase in intensity and frequency. Although mental health problems are not usually related to the Brow Chakra, I have included them in this section because when a person lacks direction they often become anxious about making decisions and fearful for the future. In many cases, some degree of anxiety and depression can follow, especially when a person begins to feel apathetic and lacks direction in life.

A person with a well-balanced Brow Chakra

- Makes quality decisions
- Seeks balance and harmony within

- Is knowledgeable and understanding, often beyond what would be expected for their age
- Has a deep spiritual awareness

CHAPTER 9: THE CROWN CHAKRA

The crown chakra is situated at the top of the head and is associated with the colour purple. When the chakra is well balanced it appears to be a deep purple with some flashes of white shining through it. When imbalanced the crown chakra appears to be much darker and dull in appearance.

This chakra is related to a person's spiritual growth, along with a person's thought processes and, when well-balanced, this chakra contributes towards clear thinking. The crown chakra is concerned with our individual relationship to God, the collective consciousness, religion, spirituality and our need for spiritual guidance. When there is an imbalance in this chakra memory is affected. A person can often live life too much in their head with lots going on in their imagination. As there is a lot going on in the head, the other senses are affected and the ability to understand other people and the world around them is affected and can lead to feelings of isolation.

For others, an imbalance can occur when they focus too much on material goods and far less on their spiritual development. When a person has a blockage in this area they end up leading a joyless life, disconnected from others around them. Such people find that they never have enough material goods and, as they acquire more and more, they become more and more unhappy.

Illnesses associated with the crown chakra

- Headaches
- Depression
- Delusional thought processes
- Aches and pains in the joints

A person with a well-balanced Crown chakra

- Enjoys a challenge in life
- Is willing to learn new things
- Has a clear understanding of themselves and their position on this earth

When the crown chakra is balanced a person feels joy in their lives. They are able to look forward to new challenges and they take the time to enjoy all that life has to offer them. Meditation, understanding one's own dreams and taking steps to develop one's own intuition will all help to balance the Crown Chakra.

CHAPTER 10: UNDERSTANDING THE AURA

WHAT IS THE AURA?

All living objects have an aura. The human energy field contains several layers which extend outwards from the human body at various distances. The seven layers of the aura relate to the emotional, physical and spiritual state of the individual. As we have a constantly fluctuating emotional state our aura changes to reflect this. Some individuals who are gifted can naturally see the colours of the aura, others need some practice.

EXERCISE: LOOKING AT SOMEONE'S AURA

Please read the whole of the section below so that you are clear what instructions you need to carry out.

The best way to do this is to ask a friend to sit with their back to a white wall in a dimly lit room.

Ensure that you have taken the time to relax and that both of you feel calm as you will not be able to concentrate if you have something on your mind.

Ask your friend to close their eyes. This will help them relax and you concentrate

Now close your eyes

Focus your attention on your Third Eye, the area between your eye brows

Take one hand and gently rub this area briefly to stimulate the Third Eye

Note: You may feel a tingling, buzzing or fuzzy sensation as you rub the Third Eye.

Now open your eyes and imagine the Third Eye opening

Focus your attention on your friend

Look at their head and shoulder area

Allow your eyes' focus to grow soft

Remember to blink gently and keep your mind clear and relaxed

Keep in this position for several minutes

When you are ready close your eyes and become aware of any background noises

Concentrate on your feet by imagining that they are firmly rooted to the ground

When you are ready ask your friend to open their eyes

Now read the section below, WHAT DID YOU SEE?

LOOKING AT YOUR OWN AURA
You can do this by looking in the mirror. Ensure that you are not going to be disturbed and try to have the mirror facing a white, or light coloured wall. Allow your eyes' focus to soften and relax. If possible find a stool or chair which you can sit on comfortably because you are going to be in this position for a while and you do not want to be distracted by your feet hurting. Remain in this seated position for several minutes. When you have finished slowly allow your senses to return to normal before you go about your day.

WHAT DID YOU SEE? Some people will find that they are only able to see a fine glow of gold or white light around the person. Other people discover that they can see bands of colours which may stay the same, or change and blend into other colours. You may see the aura some distance from the body. This happens when a person is full of life and energy as this is the sign of a healthy aura.

Perhaps you saw an aura which is close to the body, or you had a feeling that there was not very much energy present. This occurs when a person is or has been suffering with an illness. It also happens when a person has negative energy blocked within the aura.

As with most things, practice helps to improve your ability, so please do not give up if this is the first time that you have carried out this exercise and did not see very much. The more practice that you get working with different people, the more skilled you will become. It is surprising that each person's energy is so different; even more delightful is the fact that if you work with the same person several times, each time you will discover a different aura.

INTERPRETING THE COLOURS OF THE AURA

Now that you have had a chance to see the colours – what do they actually mean? Below I have listed the colours of the aura and their meaning:

White

This is the colour of someone who is highly connected to God. White indicates purity and love. A person with this colour in their aura can easily connect with angels. If there are flashes of white this means that there are angels close by.

Green

This is the colour of a natural healer. Emerald green indicates a powerful healer. However, if the colour is darker and slightly muddy, it suggests that even though that ability is present, the individual also has some degree of resentment and negative feelings which they have not dealt with and which are "stuck" in the aura.

Yellow

Pale yellow shows spiritual awareness and a connection to the Divine. Religious leaders and highly spiritual people have pale yellow auras. A bright yellow indicates that the person is struggling internally to maintain control over aspects of their lives.

Pink
A bright, clear pink shows love and compassion. I often find this colour to be present when I am teaching Reiki. At one point in the class, after a specific meditation, I can often see a number of the students with lovely, clear pink auras.

Blue
This is the colour of a good communicator. Light blue indicates a highly sensitive person who is able to freely and easily express themselves without anger or malice. A royal blue is indicative of one who is highly spiritual and can connect with the Divine.

Purple
This is a very spiritual colour. Bright purple shows that a person is able to connect with the spiritual realm. A slightly darker shade shows that a person is looking for love and desires to be connected with people on many different levels.

Orange
Indicates a person who is of a sexual nature and who is highly creative. If there is little scope for creativity in the person's life bad habits will develop as coping mechanisms, such as eating too much of the wrong type of food and smoking.

Red
This is the colour of anger, anxiety and supressed emotions. Red also shows a person who is a survivor, someone who has had a difficult life, or even someone who has been a victim of war.

Black
This indicates illness or that the person is having problems letting go of something in their past. It is also indicative of depression.

CHAPTER 11: CHAKRA CLEARING MEDITATIONS

The aim of these meditations is to cleanse and balance the chakras. Please remember that it is not the size of the chakras that is important. What is important is that the chakras are all the same size.

BEFORE YOU BEGIN

Below are some tips for you to consider before you begin your meditation.

Find somewhere quiet where you will not be disturbed as you need to concentrate on what you are doing. If you can, sit outside with nature; you will feel a great connection to the earth.

If there are other people in the household, please make sure that they are aware that you are meditating and that you should not be disturbed unless there is a genuine emergency.

You may wish to prepare the room by using candles and gentle, relaxing music.

Make sure that you have enough time to meditate. This is important because I am sure that you want to receive the full benefits of the session.

Find somewhere comfortable where you can sit with your feet flat on the ground. Remove your shoes and any socks/tights that you may be wearing. This is necessary so that any excess energy you have will go back to the earth and you will stay grounded.

You could ask a member of your family, or a friend, to read the meditation to you and you simply follow the instructions. If you do this please ask them to read the paragraph below before they begin.

Go through the meditation at least once, speaking out loud instead of reading it. It is very different speaking words rather than reading them and you need to ensure that your voice is consistent, that you pause in the correct places and that you are remembering to breathe correctly.

Alternatively, you may wish to record the meditations and play back the recordings for each of your sessions. Please consider the advice in the previous paragraph as well as the tips below which will help you:

Make sure that you carry out the recording somewhere quiet so that you do not pick up any background noise which will distract you when you listen to the recording.

Ensure that your voice is clear and evenly paced.

As you work through the meditations you will be asked to see or feel specific things. Some of you will find this easier than others. If you are quite visual, you will be able to carry out these exercises easily. You will know if you are a visual person if, for example, I asked you to think about the street you grew up in. If you can see it in your mind then you are a visual person. If you feel specific emotions then it is easier for you to experience these exercises through emotions or, perhaps, you can relate to these exercises in some other way. There is no right or wrong. Whatever works best for you really is okay. Be confident, enjoy the exercises and the experiences that you have. Remember you are unique and that is what makes you special.

Let us begin to balance the chakras and remove any negative energy. Are you ready to begin?

MORNING WAKE UP MEDITATION

This meditation is designed, as the title suggests, to awaken your body and your mind allowing you to prepare for the day ahead.

Begin by just sitting comfortably for a minute.

Focus on your breathing. Continue your natural breathing: in and out at your usual rate.

Imagine that there is a healing white light. The light enters the crown of the head and, like a laser beam, ends at the root chakra.

Focus on the light. Feel the warmth and healing energy from the light all down the centre of your body.

Now, pay attention to the **root chakra** which is situated at the base of the spine.

This chakra is a beautiful ruby red. Become aware of it as it spins and fans out.

What does your chakra look like? Is it a ruby red or does it have any areas of darkness? Perhaps it is really dull in appearance.

This chakra is concerned with your thoughts and feelings related to money and personal security.

If you feel that you have some emotions that need to be released then imagine those negative thoughts and feelings have turned into red butterflies. When you are ready release those butterflies and see them flying out from the root chakra.

Say to yourself: "I now let go of all of my worries and insecurities. I am a strong and secure person."

Now turn your attention to your to your **sacral chakra**. This is situated a few inches above the root chakra.

The colour of this chakra is orange.

Focus your attention on the sacral chakra. What do you see and feel? Do you see a beautiful bright orange with sparking light through it, or are there some areas of dullness and discolouration?

The sacral chakra is concerned with your ability to seek pleasure, joy and desire in life.

Is the sacral chakra balanced?

If you see or feel any negativity or discolouration, then imagine all of those thoughts and feelings have turned into beautiful orange butterflies.

When you are ready release those butterflies. See or feel them flying out away from your body just a few inches below your belly button.

As you release all of your negativity say to yourself: "I let go of all of my thoughts and feelings that prevent me from enjoying life."

When you are ready focus your attention on the **solar plexus chakra**. This is the area just below the rib cage.

See or feel a beautiful yellow circle of shining light. Pay attention to the solar plexus chakra. What do you see or feel? Are there dull, dark patches, or is this chakra a beautiful sunshine yellow with sparkling white light?

If you have any negative energy that you need to release imagine the energy has turned into beautiful yellow butterflies and, as you release the butterflies from the solar plexus, say to yourself: "I now release all of my fears related to self- control and control of others. All of my self-control and power lies within."

Turn your attention to your **heart chakra**.

This chakra is a beautiful green colour. What does this chakra look like? Does it have a healthy colour of emeralds with white light shining through it, or are there dull patches in this chakra?

The heart chakra is related to your concerns and feelings connected to love and relationships. Often our heart is blocked by fear.

When you are ready, release those green butterflies from your heart and out and away from your body. As you do this, say to yourself: "I now let go of all of my fears. I am free to give and receive love."

When you are ready turn your attention to your **throat chakra**.

This chakra is a beautiful light blue with streaks of white light shining through it.

What do you see/feel in this area? The throat chakra is concerned with your attitude and ability in the area of communication. Are you able to communicate freely?

Do you feel that this chakra is balanced? Are there any areas of darkness or discolouration?

If you feel that there are any emotions that you need to release then imagine a number of beautiful blue butterflies. Release them now and, as they fly out from the throat chakra, say to yourself: "I now release all of my fear and worries related to communication. I can now communicate with confidence and clarity."

Now turn your attention to your **brow chakra/ Third Eye**. This chakra is found in between the eyebrows and is concerned with your clairvoyance; your ability to see clearly, based on the understanding that all of the information that you require is found within.

The colour of this chakra is indigo. Focus on this chakra. Can you see any dull or dark patches?

If you find that there are areas of dullness/ negativity then imagine that there are a number of indigo butterflies flying out from the Third Eye. As the butterflies are released, say to yourself: "I now trust in my intuitive abilities and will look within in order to find answers to my questions."

Finally, let us turn our attention to the **crown chakra**.

The crown chakra is concerned with your purpose in life, your spirituality and your connection to the Universe.

Examine your crown chakra. Is it a lovely, even shade of purple or is it dull or dark in appearance?

If you need to release any negative energy, then imagine a number of purple butterflies flying from the crown of your head and away from your body.

As you imagine this, say to yourself: "I now release any negative emotions that prevent me from following my true path in life."

Now you have worked through the whole of the main chakra system.

When you are ready, take a deep breath and as you exhale allow the laser beam of light to fade away.

Feel your feet firmly connected to the floor.

Take a moment to be thankful for all that you have. Being grateful raises the vibrational frequency of your body and when you do this you are more able to cope with any challenges that are presented to you throughout the day.

Take your time now, slowly wake up and, when you are ready, begin your day.

EVENING THOUGHT BUBBLE MEDITATION

This meditation allows you to release any negative thoughts and feelings that have built up over the day. You will feel more relaxed and calm as you release emotions and negative feelings that have accumulated throughout the day.

Go to your quiet place and sit and relax.

Allow your breathing to continue at its usual rate.

Imagine now that your body is surrounded by a bubble of white light. You are protected by this bubble. You are safe and warm and relaxed.

Now turn your attention to your **root chakra**.

Is the chakra a lovely shade of ruby red?

How has your day been? Have you had any challenges related to your safety and personal security?

If you feel that you need to release any thoughts and feelings related to your personal security then now is the time to do so.

I want you to imagine that those negative thoughts and feelings have turned into tiny red bubbles.

Take a deep breath in through your nose.

As you exhale release those red bubbles from the root chakra.

As the bubbles are released they float down to the ground where they disappear.

Now relax and continue breathing at your usual pace.

When you are ready turn your attention to your **sacral chakra**.

Is this chakra a magnificent orange? Do you see any dull or dark patches? How has your day been? Have you had time for yourself? Have you had a chance to laugh or do something that you enjoy, or has your ability to receive pleasure in life been compromised?

If you feel that you need to release any negativity in this area then take a deep breath in through your nose.

As you exhale imagine lots of orange bubbles appearing from the area just below the belly button.

Allow the bubbles to float down to the ground where they disappear.

Now allow your attention to turn to the **solar plexus chakra**.

Do you see a beautiful yellow chakra, or are there dark or dull patches in it?

If the chakra is imbalanced why do you think this is?

Have you had difficulty maintaining self-control, either at home or at work or somewhere else? Perhaps you have problems with trying to control others, or maybe your job does entail directing and controlling others but you find this difficult? Whatever the difficulty in this area, you can now release those thoughts and feelings.

Imagine that there are lots and lots of yellow bubbles floating out through the solar plexus area. All of those bubbles contain all of your thoughts and worries related to power and control over others and your ability to maintain power and control from within.

When you are ready turn your attention to your **heart chakra**.

Does the chakra appear as a wonderful shade of emerald green or is it a little dull?

Think about your day. Have you made decisions which are right for you from your heart? Do you feel good about what has happened today?

If you feel that you need to release any emotions from the heart then imagine lots of tiny green bubbles floating down towards the ground; each bubble carrying away from your body the negative thoughts and feelings that you have experienced today.

Now turn your attention to your **throat chakra**.

Is this chakra a beautiful shade of light blue or are there dull or dark patches within it?

Have you had any difficulty communicating today, or have you had to engage in some difficult communication?

If you need to release any negativity in this area then imagine lots of small blue bubbles floating down from the throat area all the way to the ground where they disappear before your eyes.

Now turn your attention to the **Brow Chakra**.

Does this chakra appear to be healthy?

Is the chakra a shining indigo colour?

If you feel that the chakra is dull or dark, is this because you have not worked with your intuition in order to make decisions throughout the day?

If you need to release any negativity from the Brow Chakra, imagine lots of indigo bubbles floating away from the brow chakra, far away from your body and to the ground where they each simply melt away.

Finally, turn your attention to the **crown chakra**.

Is the chakra a beautiful shade of purple or does it contain some dark or dull patches?

Have you been focused on meaningful tasks today which are right for you and which are connected to your purpose in life? Has something happened today which will take you away from your purpose in life?

If you feel that you need to release any negativity from the crown chakra then I want you to imagine lots of tiny bubbles, each one containing negative thoughts and feelings related to the crown chakra. Now imagine those bubbles slowly drifting down your body to the ground where they disappear forever.

You have now worked through your main chakras system.

Take a few minutes to think about your day.

Is the something that you could or should have done differently?

Be grateful for the day that has just passed and any lessons learnt.

Allow the bubble of healing light to slowly disappear.

When you are ready, remind yourself that you are entitled to a peaceful night's sleep and that you will awaken refreshed, relaxed and looking forward to the day ahead.

OPEN YOUR HEART: CHAKRA CLEARING MEDITATION

Make yourself comfortable and, when you are ready, take a deep breath in through your nose and, as you exhale, say to yourself "relax".

Repeat the above process three times and each time you do this you will become more and more relaxed.

Focus your attention on the area around your heart.

Imagine a beautiful, warm, green healing light in the heart area.

Take a minute to think about the physical functions of the heart. The heart pumps blood all around the body. The heart is your friend as it keeps you alive. When you have done too much your heart will tell you by beating stronger and faster; when you are afraid your heart will do the same. Your heart acts as a warning system by telling you when something is wrong. Learn to listen and trust it.

Focus once more on the light around the heart.

The light now turns white, this is healing energy and this light enters your physical body around the area of the heart.

The healing light is warm and protective.

I want you to begin by thinking about your past.

Think of any event or emotion that brought sadness and negative feelings into your life.

Now I want you to let go of any residual emotions from the past that may be preventing you from moving forward with your life.

As you let go you feel those emotions, which may be strong at times, simply lift up and float into the ether where they disappear.

You can stay in this position for as long as you need, as only you know when it is time to move forward with this meditation.

When you are ready, take a deep breath in through your nose and exhale through your mouth.

I want you to think about any part of your life that you want, or need, to change. This includes things, or people, that do not bring joy into your life.

Be honest with yourself.

Some of the things that you need to change could be quite small and others may require a lot of effort and energy.

Remind yourself that you are honest and capable of making changes.

Remind yourself that you are brave and courageous and that feelings of courage arise in the heart.

Now turn your attention to all of the things that you are grateful for. I want you to say out loud all of the things that you feel gratitude for at this time.

I have listed some of the things that you may be grateful for below to help you get started. Some of the list below may not be applicable to you, please create your own as it will be more meaningful.

I am grateful for:

- Family and friends
- My health
- My job or skills
- My home
- You may wish to be grateful to a particular person who has had an impact on your life
- My body and in particular my heart

When you are grateful your vibrational frequency of your entire body, including your heart, expands and, as it does so, your heart fills with love. This is the highest vibration. When you feel love in your heart there is no space for negativity and your chakras will become balanced.

When you are ready, take a deep breath and as you exhale you notice that the light has now fully entered your heart and you feel a wonderful sense of joy and peace from within.

Now take a deep breath and as you exhale I want you to become more aware of your environment.

Feel your feet firmly rooted to the ground. You feel happier, clearer and brighter than you have for a very long time.

When you are ready you can go about your day. As you do so, you will remember all of the things that you have chosen to change or let go of and you will have the courage to begin the process today.

DEVELOPING YOUR INTUITION

Sitting in your special place for meditation, allow your body to relax for a couple of minutes as you enjoy the silence all around you.

When you are ready, imagine that there is a gentle indigo light that enters the top of your head and travels, like a laser beam, all the way down to the Third Eye which is located between the eye brows.

When you sense or feel this energy I want you to focus on your Third Eye.

Does the Third Eye feel closed or open?

In your mind if the Third Eye is closed I want you to imagine that you are opening it. You do this in the same way that you would if you were to open your other eyes.

As it opens, you may feel a tingling or buzzing sensation around the area of the Third Eye.

Now that the Third Eye has opened allow the indigo light to expand until it fills the whole of your head and connects with the Crown Chakra.

Imagine that the indigo energy and light is cleansing and balancing the Brow and Crown chakras as it makes small, gentle, circular movements.

As the light circles and passes through the chakras it removes any negative energy and dark patches.

When you feel that both chakras have been cleared, hold the light in your head as you say the following affirmations out loud:

"My Third Eye has now opened and expanded so that I can see all that there is to see.

I understand that the answers to my questions lie within and I may need to work with my subconscious mind in order to find the answers to my questions.

I understand that there is no other reality other than that which I create myself.

I will listen to the messages that my higher self, my guides and angels send me in order to live my life for the highest good."

When you are ready take a deep breath in through your nose.

Hold this breath for a few seconds.

As you exhale I want you to release the light and energy and when you are ready you can go about your day feeling relaxed and refreshed.

CLEARING YOUR AURA OF NEGATIVE ENERGY

This is an important exercise because a lot of negative energy can become trapped within the aura, affecting the mental and spiritual well-being of a person. This exercise can be carried out whenever the need arises. I do suggest though, when you first begin to carry out the chakra clearing exercises, you carry this exercise out once or twice a week. This will ensure that you are really removing negative and harmful energy from your body.

Sit quietly for a moment or two.

Become aware of your aura. There are seven layers of the aura but for this exercise you do not need to concern yourself with each individual layer.

Focus your attention on your aura. Imagine that the aura has expanded all around your body.

Now, imagine a carbon copy of yourself is standing behind you.

This carbon copy is holding a clear quartz crystal wand in their right hand.

Starting at the top of the head, the carbon copy begins by making small circular movements which travel all the way down the right side of your body.

The small circular movements lift and remove any negativity which has become stuck in your aura.

Once the right side of the body has been done, the carbon copy continues all the way up the left side of the body until it reaches the head.

The carbon copy now disappears.

You now imagine a beautiful white healing light begin at your heart.

The energy begins to move out and expand through your entire body.

The energy now begins to work through the auric field.

The aura expands further and further into the room.

You feel the vibrational frequency of your body increase.

Now you feel a loving and deep connection to all of nature.

You feel at peace and very relaxed.

You now know that your aura has been cleansed.

When you are ready you can imagine your aura returning to its natural position.

Tip: If you wish to send love and healing energy, imagine the aura expand and fill the room. Just like a bird or angel spreading its wings you can expand your aura and send love and healing light to others. This is a wonderful gift that really makes a difference.

ETHERIC CORD CUTTING

If you feel a deep emotional attachment to a person which is having a negative impact on your mental, physical and spiritual health you need to carry out the Etheric Cord Cutting process. Etheric cords are like thick tubes or pipes connecting us to other people to whom we have a strong connection such as our parents, brothers and sisters, other relatives and people with whom we have had a sexual relationship. We also form attachments with people who have had a strong influence on our lives.

Below I have listed some examples of when the cord cutting process is necessary:

If you keep thinking about another person and these thoughts are upsetting.

If you have been in a previous relationship that has ended suddenly or badly and you are unable to move on with life.

You keep making the same mistakes in life and feel unable to move on.

You feel connected to a place, such as your home or work environment, and on a conscious level want to move somewhere else but feel connected to the place and are unable to.

THE CORD CUTTING PROCESS

Go to your usual place of meditation.

Allow your body to relax and take a few deep breaths in and out.

Now imagine a carbon copy of yourself standing at the side of you holding a white sword.

You may wish to call upon the angels to help you with this process, such as Archangel Michael.

If you do this imagine that the angel is standing behind you, holding your hand with the sword in it – this is to empower and support you.

Now begin the process of cord cutting.

You will be guided by your intuition as to where the cord needs to be cut.

The cord is best cut with a quick and purposeful movement.

When you cut the cord, imagine that you are releasing the connection to the person or place that has been blocking your energy and which has prevented you from moving forward with your life.

With all of your senses feel the cord being cut, release the emotion and let go.

Where do I need to cut the cords?
You should work using your intuition combined with the information held in your conscious mind. If you feel that you want to move from a particular place then cut the cords around your feet.

If you feel a lot of emotion from the heart then cut the cords extending from the heart chakra.

If you feel that your spiritual development has been affected then cut the cords extending from the Third Eye chakra.

If you feel that a connection to a person had led to physical insecurities and money worries then cut the cord at the root chakra.

Continue to do this process for as long as you feel it is necessary.

When you feel that the process is complete, thank any angel that has assisted with this task.

Allow the visualisation of the carbon copy of yourself, along with sword, to disappear.

Take a deep breath and relax.

You will notice a physical difference. You will feel lighter and more refreshed and relaxed. You are now free to live your life as you wish and to continue on your own path and not one which has been created, or blocked, by another person.

If you have enjoyed reading this book you may also be interested in other books by Marion McGeough:

Crystal energy healing: Chakras, Pendulums, Wands

A Beginner's Guide to Crystal Healing & the Five Elements of Traditional Chinese medicine

A Beginner's Guide to developing your intuition: Discover how you can use your senses to guide you

A Beginner's Guide to Mindfulness: Achieve peace with each step you take

Shoden: The definitive guide to first degree Reiki: Mindfulness, Meditation, Reiki treatments and more.

A Beginner's Guide to the Chakras

Crystal Healing and the Human Energy Field: A Beginners Guide

Hypnosis CD
Overcome Your Fear of Flying

All products available from Amazon

If you have enjoyed reading this book you may be interested in studying my Crystal Healing course and Reiki courses. Further details can be found by going to www.britishacademyofreiki.co.uk

NOTES:

NOTES:

Printed in Great Britain
by Amazon

50055124R00056